April 2016
Martin, old
as a path
wilderness of my bewilderment,
something the vultures couldn't
eat up. G Bennett Myers

Across Time

Grady Bennett Myers, Jr.

Cover and interior design by Sable Books
Cover & interior art by Mary Alice Griffin Myers

Editor: Raleigh David Myers
Literary Consultant: Ruth Moose
Author photograph: Lou Lipsitz
Additional art photography: Wayne Morris Photography

Sable Books
sablebooks.org

Contents

For my family past and present

For the men of the Men's Center
who believed in and supported me
and my poetry from the beginning

The University of North Carolina at Chapel Hill

New Hampshire

Across Time

Across Time

Across the street
Across time   the river
The sky   time again
There is no almost

The woman at the window
She'll keep looking
She knows there's no return
She does it anyway

It's a feast of what was
Don't let it go
The mind has made
A safe place for it.

Windows

I came from a family
That didn't have any
Well   maybe they
Were just shuttered

Bars   no
You could look out

Everybody had one
Mine was the upstairs bathroom
I could see Pilot Mountain
Out my window

My soul had a window
I didn't want any looking in

I was an upstairs boy
I became an upstairs man
To look out   see them
Not seeing me

Sometimes I want to touch.

Windows II

An upstairs window guy
Yes
See but not touch
Nor hear   yes

It's like watching a silent movie
Without the sub-titles
I must imagine

They look like those French
Impressionist paintings
Maybe a *Seurat*
Walking a dog

Children-a-scurry
Don't know where they're running
Theirs is a
Nothing makes a difference
Just a matter of energy afloat

Sometimes I wonder
If they
Stare at me staring at them

Once walking the streets of New York
Maury said stop staring
It's dangerous to look into people's eyes

Late my years
I look for eyes
For their color
Especially blue

Literature makes extravagant
Attributions to eye language
Tolstoy says eyes tell all
I don't know
I keep looking but I don't yet see.

Windows III

If you write to a Death Row prisoner
His name will be Jimmy
When you get enough courage
You'll visit   Sit on a backless stool
In a phone booth size cubicle
Overcome by thick concrete walls
Heavy as lead   Strain to see his
Smiling black face and beautiful
White teeth   through the inch -
Thick chicken-wire glass
The size of a box of Nabisco crackers
I wept   Jesus wept for Lazarus
He could raise him from the dead
They want to kill Jimmy
I am no match for the power of State.

Windowlights

I, a scribe
All alone
Peeping into my mind's lust

I, have a calling
Write it down
Weave a word basket

Writing, it's a wound
Step out on a thin hair of disbelief
No net below

I am the net
I cry
Too real, too close, no exit

The net
You are my net
I am caught
I like it

The yin and the yang
Alone and together
Alone creates
Together I'm nourished, excited
Blessed.

The Construction Of Time

Old men and children are close
The young have just come
The old are soon going there
They can stand and watch all day
Watch men with hammer and bulldozer
A new building.

Old men on park benches and fishing piers
They don't say much
They don't have to
It's the young who talk

Old men and babies are quiet
Babies absorb it all
They cry if they hurt
Old men hurt and don't cry

They are between a world that rises
And one that falls
They have an agenda
Which is another way to
Say beginning middle and end

When I am one of the old men
I will take my stand
To watch the will of the world
I want to be in line

Waiting to see what the world is doing
I will have a button to push
To stop it if it moves too fast

The children and I can
Look for a while and
They won't have to grow up.

Unfinished

I wonder if I am coming
Back to where I am

If I am part of the grass
That packs a hillside
Or a lowly cucumber

Division comes easier than reunion
Putting myself together
Is a lifetime

Adam and Eve are still unfinished.

Time Recycled

Brown baggy oak leaves
Cling to their parent branches.
The November winds
Have not blown them away.

Suspended in time
Are they to drop of their will
Or be pushed by new buds?

Time is like that
Just waiting to be dropped away.
And where does used time go
To some far away black hole.
It'll be laundered
Hung out to dry.

Look up on a sunny day
Against a blue sky
White billowy clouds
Your Time recycled.

Take the Old Road

From Chapel Hill to Durham
Take the old road
The Indians did
Their trading path
You can see the old road
Ruts in the woods

Barns aplenty populate this road
Half-hidden behind
Almost every dwelling
Whether a small farmhouse

Or a recent brick ranch
Where past cultures
And today's economies
Have saved a rural marriage

Here you can see
Chicken hens-a-scratch
Today's wash hangs the line
White sheets flap in the wind

An old board-and-batten barn
Hugging close to the road
Leaning painfully   says
Please help me   I'm falling

Cows in the pasture
Acres and acres of green
Behind barbed wire
And cedar hedgerows

A brick Baptist church
In front of its well-clipped cemetery
Granite stones stand to recall

By now you know you're
In democracy as Southern
As spreading mayonnaise
On white bread
For a tomato sandwich

You'll have to drive slowly
To see the retired
Log tobacco barns and corncribs

Three wild turkey hens
And a gobbler preening
All the feathers of his ego

Down a crepe myrtle alley
The nineteenth century white
Federal manor house rests
Behind cedars and English boxwoods

The lord of the manor
A good neighbor because
He's been dead a hundred years

The caretaker keeps the large
Lawns mowed   shrubbery trimmed
Raises flags   when the family
Returns   Awaiting the lord

Beyond the horse pasture
Way down the road
To the big cypress swamp

Where earth air sky
Water and wood meet
The vortex
From which we all sprang

With mutual respect and dignity
You'll remember this road
It is a memory of time.

Griffin Islands Road

The swamps and islands and pocosins
If they are not your world
As they are not mine

You need a password
And a mind that is subject to the animal
Residents of two legs, four, wings
Scales and slippery circuitous sliders
On their belly that hiss or rattle

Yet you make me want you
Griffin Islands Road
You put me to the test
And let me know
What I must leave behind

That drive down the dark road
Wants to suck me in
Swamp calls my name

Murky dark waters are slow
They take me on their way
Hung by parasitic vines
Spanish Moss   come up for
Air like a cypress knee

Murky dark water
The swamp cannot have me
As much as I cannot have it

My home is over the hills
That grew me
Hills put up blinders
That keep me from seeing far
Enough to go anywhere else.

The Language of Pickup Truck

I don't speak the language of pickup truck
have never been surrounded by an army
of pickup trucks but they give me a safe
and secure feeling like
the wagons circling around

at the gathering of family and society
where the wide open is brought near
in the flat lands of empty cotton fields
usually miles from me   where I see the
detritus of white fluff the cotton picker
dropped.

The fallow fields are smooth clean
for a winter waiting quiet rest to companion
the pickup truck congregation surrounding
the big white tent of pig-picking barbecue fried
oyster shrimp brunswick stew hushpuppy event

with grace and mutuality that blends the
know-each-other language there
perpetuates itself like cooking with gas
to fry the oysters fish hushpuppy
in the pickup truck voice of a marriage
that will last as long as it lasts.

La Maison Ecoutant

If the street bends and rises
To a generous white house
That's looking at you
It'll say come on 'round back
We know you

Past the old barn
They call it the garage
It will tell you
Of a day when the horses

Back door lets you in
To the big radiator
That's going to hiss at you

Kitchen can't show you
The old wood stove
But you will see the chimney
Standing like a sculpture

Of sun dried brick
Set off by the smile of mortar
White as an angel's wing

This old house does not apologize
Thinks more about change than does it
Believes in wasted space
Looks up doesn't give a spit
About dropped ceilings

Dining room will seat you
At the round mahogany table
It sips sweet tea with lemon
Eats strawberry shortcake
With whipped cream

That's what stories are like
When they're listened to   and
Take on the sacredness of sacrament
Like you would Sunday afternoon sit

In front porch rockers
And abide the treasure
Of being together
While the world out there
Is in its place.

Voice

The song of the South I know
A slow pileated drawl
About the consistency of egg custard

Now gone

The human voice I can still hear
The awe of tongues resounding in my ear

The things that are gone are nearest.

stuck in second

out of low
hesitate briefly
in neutral

before second
pick up speed
to move to high

it's standard shift
but he's not
up to standard

everybody else
is driving hydramatic

you know what

he slips back
through neutral
lands in second

and lives
a pissed-off life

squinting
to see
out of
the cracked windshield.

artist

she's painting
how could she
all those relations
hanging on
her right arm

what if what if
you shook them off
would there
be any paint
left in you

here I am
staring at the paint
it's your flesh
hangs on the canvas

paint's not dry
the brush in
your right hand
the painting's unfinished.

Herring Roe and The Cypress Grill

Safely over sixty
Five riders of wheels
All men save one woman
In a purple tee shirt
They wore leather chaps
Head over heels all black
Gloves jeans helmets
They had a rhythm
Like costumed ballet dancers
Filing on stage for their performance.

They'd wheeled into the Cypress Grill
River Roanoke's herring season wonder shack
Half ready to finish sliding into a river
Not to be fooled by the lacy Spanish moss
The seething deep dark waters
A current ready to suck everything in
For its own pleasure.

The cafe is safe inside
The sign reads no alcohol and no nonsense
Beside its Grade A rating
The age-stained plank walls
Unharmed by years of dark light
Seats all the fat men for lunch
Eating fried roe
Slaw stewed potatoes herring hushpuppies
And finally, guaranteed to
Hold a working man until suppertime
A piece of pecan pie
They make from local nuts.

Outside, brighter than the sun
More chrome than Detroit
Over-decorated over-gadgeted
Over-polished heavyweights
Five Harley-Davidsons
waiting for their masters.

Liver and Onions

Couldn't get that taste out of my mouth
even if I wanted to. It's gravy-smooth
creamy greasy not even lumpy
runs smooth as liquid silk over my
mashed potatoes but not smothering
the green beans.

Foods know what connects what
and what belongs
beside the road since 1936   the last
the last diner on US 1 in Damariscotta, Maine
where you must line up for a table
for six but settle for three and
three before Paulette waitress

for twenty-three years glides up with the
confidence of ancient Jerusalem after
your meal to ask if you are ready for
your low-bush Maine blueberry or
rhubarb pie a la mode. Miss Ella has been
making pies out back for sixteen years.

On my way to the cash register
I came to myself coming to me.
I could see the criss-cross
of America seated in booths

with arms on tables where
the nation met itself as equal
or unequal as entering a voting booth.

I paid the bill at the cash register
and picked up a magnetic refrigerator placard
for my best friend in
Chapel Hill that says
"Pie Fixes Everything."

Chicago and Me

In the shadow of Calder's steel
A statue I named no-man
The giant that guarded Windy City
Allowed the mercury to flop to zero

Trying not to get blown over
By the Chicago I discovered
When 1965 was today
My window in the Conrad Hilton
Said   Look out at Lake Michigan

Art Institute raptured me with fine paintings
But said politely don't put
Fingerprints on the white marble statue

Marshall Field said come on in
Our big after Xmas sale
Thirty floors of clothes furs beds boots
All I got was mark-down
Pima cotton boxer shorts

Four pairs over-the-calf cashmere sox
Blue black beige brown
I don't know how long
Kashmir goats live
Nor the herdsmen who shear the wool

Winter feet want to be warm
I'm still wearing the socks
Worn thin but not worn out
I wipe the dirt off my windshield
With those Egyptian cotton boxer shorts.

Cutaway

I feel like a classic Cadillac
I am a classic
Everything about me is vintage now
I can afford to leak.

I run my own pace
Be my own bishop and
Preside over my history
Like an owl

Sitting on a limb
Looking out on a world
He doesn't have to consult
Hoot.

Hawk

I'll fly if I'm a hawk
Interrupt my lazy kettle
and zoom in on my prey
With never an ethical thought

I'll look up to God
And say yes
Leave a pile of fur
Where the mouse was
Let the ants feast on cleanup

But I have two enemies
Hunger and blue jays
Though I am much bigger
Small birds tease me from behind

I've been called a chicken hawk
There's nothing chicken about me
Can you bear to look at my talons
And not shudder

Or that slice-it-thin beak
My plumage blends so naturally
You don't see my shadow
In the tree

But my piercing eyes see
Right through you
And will scare a man.

Eagle

What right has my speeding car
To interrupt a giant eagle
Ripping his road kill
With razor sharp beak
And steel studded talons

I'd never seen an eagle
Glimpsed only his
Gray feathery breast
Squatting beside the road

Each startled by the other
Confronted with the invasion
Of my Sunday afternoon ride

Through his Shenandoah Valley
But his eyes faster than mine
He was gone in sudden flight

I never saw him again
Any more than he saw me.

Found

Tools, my best lifted from road kill
A pair of adjustable pliers that look
Like a crow with a big beak and
Long tail hanging down

A forged steel open-end
Adjustable monkey wrench
A heavy stainless steel pair of pliers
With blue plastic sleeves on the handles

The heaviest thing I ever found
Was a log chain coiled
Like a snake on the road in Spring Lake
It went to my wife's nephew
He's a serious Down East farmer

The lightest thing was a delicate fourteen karat
Gold bracelet in the parking lot of
The Cross Creek Mall. I find
More precious metals in my recurring dreams
Silver fifty-cent pieces I pick up
The more I take the more silver coins I find

Found an extra twenty dollars
In my hand from a bank teller
In Salem, Oregon in 1958
No, I gave it back

In 1972 I found a twenty on the floor of
A drug store in Floyd, Virginia
I have stooped to pick up a
Plethora of ball point pens
Some write and some don't.

Dog Smiles

Would that I a dog could be
Surely a long hair
Big as a lion
In the back of my master's
Pick-up truck
Head held high
Ears a-flying
Looking out on the world
Proving that dogs can smile.

I'd ride like Haile Selassie
The lion of Judah
Rode his chariot around Ethiopia
In full command
Of his thousand year reign.

I'd stick my head in
Through that truck window
And give my owner a slobbery lick.

Never mind
He reaches back
Gives an approving pat on the head
And the world turns around
One more time.

A Short History of Cats That Does Not Include All Their Nine Lives

July days are not exceptional
But one was the strangest ever
That was the day the lights went out
The whole world died
Nobody left to explain why
Argue about it   Conduct last rites
Nor to call the electrician.

Nothing left but cats
Cats
They didn't mind
Living happily ever after.

Until one day in the forest
A stray pushed a gnarl of a button
On a tree
Started the whole thing all over again
Here we are.

The Last Shade-Tree Mechanic

You can almost see through the opaque
of the grove of trees down the road
to the polity of his sanctuary

Shade tree mechanics   you must understand
you can't find their definition in the dictionary
nor the census because they didn't graduate
from high school and he is not an ordained
priest from General Motors Training Institute

His is not your language   His greasy words
are caster camber magneto differential

and his independence doesn't care about
your ignorance   His gaze is on the'88 Buick
he has lifted by a block and tackle and log chain

over an oak limb thick as your thigh
His is time more valuable than yours
empties the quart motor oil can
that he saved as a spitoon

He is the savior of many things
and much is saved in him

He picks up his socket wrench
They join hands
to do what they do.

Rust

Her Cadillac has holes in it
The lord of nature rust
His lover oxygen

Two hundred thousand miles
Of meals   Rust eats
Car flesh of Cadillacs
Queen of the king's highway

Queen of the road
Body by Fisher 1978
All the grace of the
Route to the stars

Fins like God gave every fish
To guide to glide
Now rust her fine fins clipped
Rust of the road

Where God meets us coming back
From where we've been so long
The Cadillac hostess with holes

Two hundred thousand miles
Body by Fisher 1978
Great fins went first

Lord of nature rust.

Rooms

Every time I hear about hell fire
It burns some of me
Part of it is me
And part the Book in my body

Some is God in me
Some is demon gods
Stone-carved gods of shame

But the restless in me
Ready to get out
Like a butterfly
In a cocoon

Perhaps I should could
Settle myself inside
Those houses of self
Bastions battlements

Like rooms in a castle
A place for shame
A room for grace
One for hate
One for the piety of hate.

Projection

Like awaiting rain in a dry time
The sovereign sitting somewhere
In a black hole resting
God gets so much projected on Him

The thunder I hear
Some say that is God talking
Some call man the wounds of God
Jesus called Himself the Son of God
Abraham was called to give his son to God

Priests try to talk to God
Prophets speak for God
Preachers speak God to men

Heaven is like a second story porch
They always have railings so no one will fall
While the guests sit around rocking
At the mountain inn that has a view to forever

I think God got tired of naming things
He needs the seventh day respite
As he had after a week of creative burst

He's sitting in some black hole resting now
While pondering the fate of reptiles
And the shame of men.

Shirt

When I put a shirt on I want it
to fit me and he will say
it must fit him with that
feel of his skin on mine

with fabric not shaky flimsy
silky but firm enough
that it will hold.

Let him be hand-picked
cotton broadcloth with
body   yes   but not as stiff as a
canvas tarpaulin flapping sailcloth.

A white shirt with real pearl
buttons he knows when and where
the need to wear one.

Blue shirt button-down
is a man with
that mutual come to me touch.
We know we belong.

Woodex

The South in a box
From the war
Slaves in that empty box

I come here in the wood walls
Of my mind
Age-stained heart pine
Aromatic cedar of red

Southerners had cedar chests
Stuffed with hope
Kept moths and flying things out
Secrets locked in
I got out

My final box
Pine
I'm filling it
As poets do
It'll hold me
And my memories

But for now my friends
I have no secrets
I am yours.

Shadow

If you are going to bring a
piece of shadow to light
you have to break it off and
let it be in the safety of friends

as if it is ever safe as if shadow
is safe It won't go back
with its jagged edges because
shadow's perimeter always re-seals

A no-return of merchandise
policy even with a receipt
I shiver and shake and shame

There's no way out
There's no way in
It's Don Quixote all over again
Life is consequence.

Passage I

She was the verb
The passion
The water over the falls.

Over and over
The swollen river
Seeking banks it could not find.

The conflict was between
The is and the seem
The is was never enough
The seem was so fair
But always so far.

Now the flooding is over
The river knows its bounds
We leave it to its flow.

Ambivalence

It was solid sound I heard
And I turned to see what train.
T'was a lipstick red Dodge Ram.

She, driving his truck
She, lighting a serious king-sized cigarette
Hesitant, she, to kill the duet her dual mufflers raged.

Finally she dismounted
Yielded enough control

To enter the doctor's office.
Her body thin as a postage stamp
Years over fifty

And ambivalence over a hundred
Like a steam train
Puffing her way in.

Cry

Some say there is cry inside a rock
The cry I know is a deep guttural moan
If you are going to have one
Let it belong
In bursts of uncontrol

Lightning must be that way
It's your archetypal blessing
Don't fool with hiding it
Behind a laugh as shame insists

Cry by yourself
If you have to
Just you and the gods
They're already in you

They've had eons of cry
Falling from the sky
Pushing rocks up hills
Life is weep.

Eros

1970 photograph going down the
Hallway of my mind
The long dark seam of her hose up
From snaky spit-shined knee-high
Leather boots all the way to the
Black mini-skirt high on her thigh

Walking ahead of me in the hallway of
The mental health center the
Social worker who brought her style all the
Way from California to the East Coast

Shelved close by in the permanent
Collection in the library of my mind
The surviving shiny sepia-colored tin-type
Late nineteenth century photographs
Fragile heirlooms but they last.

Suddenly

Contains all the cloudbursts
Of Eros
So human so divine
When you remember the body
So well-made so convulsive
So Eros so un-lion-tamed
With the far-away brain
Assigned to play cop.

Where Have All The Birds Gone

For if man must live by bird alone
Then he is a dying breed
If birds beckon the night from sleep
And the nightingale calls the night

Dear God
Don't leave me
Lay down a basket
Simple split oak strips woven
Then I can gather up life

Holy writ says widows
Naomi and Ruth
Poor gleaners of the field

Boaz was rich
His baskets ran over
He gleaned Ruth
And the world's another love story
Rich marries poor

If good mated with evil
Who's the offspring
Who am I the son of
Like the Greek gods

Always condemned to something forever
Am I sentenced to the eternal life of ponder
Am I more of God
Or more of evil

And my sister said we have
Fewer birds this year.

Grandpa Bailey

Papa
That's the name I hear
Walter Fletcher Bailey
As I am awakened   in my straw-tick bed
He's chunking the fireplace downstairs.
Every day he woke the sleeping sun
And told it to shine and work.

He worried the creek's going to rise
Get his corn in the bottom lands
But Papa got the corn, not the creek
And sold it peddling vegetables in town.
When he died he had $27,000 on deposit,
Four houses, 120 acres, and a pickup truck
But no running water.

Grandma Bailey   She won't tell you.
She's a little woman
She does just four things
Smile, in her rocking chair
Cook twenty-one meals a week
Including Sunday night supper
Churn milk to sell butter
And make nine children.

They still use his log tobacco barns
And farm his one acre fenced garden.
The muddy farm road remains
One-fourth mile of bumpety potholes
Papa filled with broken Pine Hall brick.

They've burned the white house down
Two hundred years old.
Where is the log barn
The corn crib
The front yard's crooked elm.
All's left is the log smoke house
That still smells of his smoke and molasses
And the well house.

Where's Grandpa
He's gone to church
He always went   and she did too
To the Moravian Graveyard
They left five generations of Moravians
I am one of those.

Grandpa's Creeks

Where two creeks don't come together
It's between them
Grandpa's hundred twenty acre farm
Could have been an island
If a creek on the fourth side

He didn't mind
Neither did the creeks
When they flooded
His bottom lands

Grandpa leaned against his
Porch post and moaned
The creek's going to get my corn

They winked at their game
Grandpa knew flood waters
Delivered flood-rich fertilizer

On his bottom lands
Potent dirt
For watermelons and corn

Boys in fast-step to big-man
Liked to steal a watermelon
Were stunned by Grandpa's shotgun

Watermelon was Grandpa's currency
Loaded on his pickup
The peddler
Headed for the bank.

Basketball Son

My son where
From fall to spring
Goes into a basketball
Inside with friends

By television and telephone
They speak from basketballs
In other states

Speak their inflated
Leather covered words
Basketball alters their state
Naturally pumped up

They deflate late in spring
He'll be back.

When Peter and I Went to Look For a Waterfall

Mountains you talk to me all the time
When I am with you
And I can never get enough
I want to listen

To every word you say
Talk and listen
You also creep up over and around me
You cover me

And I become you
I am the mountain
And I get lost in that delicious
That isn't crying

It's a total closeness to everyone
But no one can enter
The purity of that space
Other than you my son

Because I am full of you
And all and everyone
It is a moist excitement
It also lets me smell

That pungent and acrid odor of
The earth's secret recipe
To keep the fires burning
Put on another stick of wood, my son.

Winter Woods

I love to walk the winter woods.
They make me look up.
Tall trees say tall things.
They may even talk to God
Since they are higher than anything
Reaching up to grab the first light
Where they always seem to whisper.

Down here if I look straight ahead
I can see a long way
Through the barren woods
Sometimes they share inner secrets
After summer leaves depart.

That's when I walk at will
Until a hanging vine stops me
Or I step into a hidden hole.
Those clinging vines and hidden holes
Help to keep me humble.

Heart Pine

I saw a whole forest
Laid out
On the back of a trailer truck
Two by tens
Not saying a word
I cried

They could be my ancestors
Maybe that's why I love trees
I already wrote one poem on my family tree

I probably sprang from a hollow log
Severed my umbilicus from a tree root
I count my family in board feet.

Good Morrow Woods

Good Morrow Woods
You seem glad to see me
You've put on your best today

Your dress is always perfection
Somehow it's no matter
Even if you're naked in winter
Or in your blossomy best spring outfit

All my life I've sheltered with you
Everything goes back to you
Sometimes I feel like you want me
Especially if I get lost in the woods

I never see those holes I fall into
I wonder if you are trying to take me back
Maybe I came from you
Just on loan to the world.

Swamp Maples

Swamp maples
You
Gray throated
Neck of red

Tell it first
Expel the secret
Of sap on the rise

Swamp maples
Throat is gray
Neck is red

Never could keep a secret
Sap did it to you again
First
And now the world knows

It's spring.

Redbud

From winter woods
Opening the curtains
Just at the sun-seeking edge
Redbud   peeks out

Subtle and delicate
Like lace
From the crochet
Of Breton women
Just for the dance of the ballerinas

The wind   Graceful
Blowing the branches
Makes the swirl of the dance
That celebrates the ritual
Spring   sap on the rise

Finale   The red costumes fade
Come the leaves
To curtain the close of the dance.

Scrub Oak

The scrub oak there when
we built fourteen years ago
about the height of the nipple
on my chest I said
chop chop No she said

Today is mid-October
Leaves are yellowing
sixty feet high and growing

Tree and me I was a scrubby
had to fight for a place
felt forced to bear fruit
to avoid being marginalized

Always on the edge
counting my rings
My trunk's
now past its prime

A tree calculates its life in rings
has a long-time contract
with the universe for the
care and feeding of its rings

The measure of my life
is those who care
about adding rings
to my trunk.

The Blue Table

La table says that crossroad of history between the
New Hampshire cabinetmaker, New England,
Charles Van Rensselaer, Antiques Barn, and me.
The table is a shy sky blue badly bruised paint
Adopted for $20 in Hopkinton Center, New Hampshire in 1965.

Charles Van Rensselaer was tall, gray, wore custom-made jump suits
Came across like someone appearing around a corner
He was one of the last of those New York Dutch aristocrats
Had parceled out his fortune on his several wives
Was a charmer with a sort of bitter humor
Reminded me of the writings of D. H. Lawrence.

The taper legged lightstand
No drawer, maple, modest charm, says little, but
Talks to me on the underside
You can feel his hand-drawn rive marks
Like that rock-ribbed New England coastline
The surface, the exterior so perfectly smoothed
It covers those rocky Yankees
Their words spare in telling it   but

Their subtle warmth won me over, and
That too was an adoption
This table and me, it holds its mortised secrets
No nails, no pegs, just thirty two glue blocks
A perfect architectural gem
It's the mind of that nineteenth century cabinetmaker
Became flesh and holds the table and me together.

North Creek Farm

If you're going to have a store
It'll be in your home
Hidden by the great tall bushes
Call it North Creek Farm

Attached barn   walk in on
Wide pine floor   uneven stumble
Over twenty-penny nails oozing
Out of age-worn boards

Like the stories of the feet of
Horses and men stepping into the
Barn's secrets now spread out
Before you in tempting wares

That offer what two good hands
Rend from the smiles on God's
Green earth   jams of raspberry
Big fat cookies   handmade soaps

Unique garden tools seed packets
Dried flowers and herbs hang the
Hand-hewn beams   saying take me home
To soups stews

Eat here in Suzanne's café
Organics grown in the back
Where chickens scratch among
Heirloom roses perennials vegetables

You can take from this place
That eats you up   spits you out
And you'll dance your way home.

God Man Moose Maine

It was God calling taps
To close the day
Taking His sun
Out the world's western gate
Reflecting red on Mount Washington's snow
A hundred miles away

Bull moose with a lyrical lope
Down Dick's road
Staring at us
Big as a tugboat
God in a mammal

If you want to
Break up a dinner party
Just bring in a moose
But it didn't wrack the hostess
And Dick put the lobster in the pot

For four couples
Married one hundred forty years plus
Without a break.

Friends

If you are going to have friends,
Let them be long time,
And if they are rich enough
To own part of the ocean,
Let them be as generous
As they are rich.

We know how to eat
Off each other's plates and
Because of years this can be.
We know each other's black box,
Where the dust curls are,
And the broom.

The tattoo of time has imbedded,
And departures have not faded it.
Let time continue to breed
Its honeyed glue that won't wash.
Let them kiss freely
With the lips of free speech.

Yes, we've talked much of love,
And it's old enough to vote,
But you have to hold it up
Because it can't stand alone.

The Justice of Granite

The Old Man Of The Mountain
Was the watching-over
And what we thought was forever—
Crumbled.

Now a mass of rocks
He's the precious pile of granite
A memorial sacred to
Those who knew him

Every piece is solid to the touch
Would that we could be up there
Where he lives
The unfinished cathedral of the sky.

Thirty-Nine Rumford Street

She presides   The Salon
A presence as if a painting
The images hanging the walls
She   looking at the paintings
Looking back   at her

This is the reward
The awaited day has come
The piece of finality
She is the place

There is little of mystery
It is all here before you
The outside sounds can be fierce and loud
Like rebellion in the streets

But her friends know her door
The table is set
The children come
And then they can go

Family and friends
This time and this place
Has given its peace.

Café Sophia

Fifteen years parted
They met on granite
These solid women
Stepping on fifty
The trio who bore their sons of the sixties
And counter to culture
Kept their husbands and families
For the nineties

Save one
The Aussie lady
Gave her husband to heaven
Was his heart
At Heathrow Airport
Where the business of man sub-served
The business of God

Now
New Hampshire October calls leaves
The color of God
Makes ripe apples drop on your head
Makes you listen to falling maple leaves

The women
At the Café met
And measured the collected wisdom
The seethe of their forties had dealt them:
Grief, pain, scars.

For healing, their old and chattery blessing ritual:
Inspecting, correcting, directing
Their sons, daughters, friends, enemies:
And they were reconnected.

Before they took the parting ritual photo
Of their love,
These three sisters of
Sophia
Swore to write.

Now
I am the letter they vowed to send
And I am writing the pictures I took.

Love Catherine Love Chris

If you visit your friend
In her Hallmark Card Shop
Let her be a good friend
And an old one

While there if you must drink coffee
From cups that are paper
And fetch them from downstreet yourself
Let it be the best Green Mountain coffee

At her shop
If she tells you her brother died of leukemia
Let her say
Let her say he died in her home in her arms

Let his last words be
    Catherine   Help me

Her last words to him
    Chris   It's okay

His final breath the longest sigh
His mask in death
The peace of the other world.

Such A Big Man   Bartlett

To carry the name
Go to the Declaration
Of Independence   to Josiah Bartlett
And a town up north named for you

To claim it
Plow the river bottom fields
Of the Merrimac for humility
And a passion for the land

He is passion-a-plenty
More than enough
To fill a good backpack
Running over

A whole freight train of it
Don't even think of a boxcar for
Frivolity foolishness and waste
That freight is always loaded

Carries Concord Hospital   Hospice
Visiting Nurses   Boys and
Girls Club   Save the Environment
A boxcar for integrity   honesty
More than one for discipline

Another for good humor
Family and friends   but no caboose
Because there is no end to the train

I hopped this freight almost fifty
Years ago   I'm not about to
Throw myself off the train.

Dick Bartlett 75

A fork in the road
Take it to Concord
If you see a Yankee
He'll tell you

Bartlett measured
With integrity
All the land
In Merrimac Valley

Driving that faded green
'48 Studebaker he found
Abandoned in the woods
He could rest then

Take the other fork
Ask a moose
Where's Osprey Point
Unless you're in a boat
You'll be at land's end

See a white circus tent
It's not a Dick Withington
Antiques Auction

It's the Dick Bartlett Roast
To celebrate
Elder Squire, benevolent
Lord of Merrimac Valley

If you know something good
Stand and say it
Some might add a few lies

Which won't matter to him
For seventy-five years
He's been finding
The truth in life.

Sideboard

He's somebody's castoff
The back room of Boston's
Fifty Dollar antique shop
Just a leftover Empire maverick
The day of delicate proportions
He missed it

Sideboard's raw red wood
Jungle islands giant mahogany
Sawn planed joined
The cabinetmaker's skilled hands

Drawer front streaks of black
Run parallel lines back and forth
Like swimmers in a race

Interrupted at the top drawers
Crotch veneers swirling
Like the dance of ballerinas

The weight of sideboard's posture
So stable subtle silent
Makes me want to break
Out some human cry
I think he'd understand

This quiet beast just sits
Wisely as wood does
Being himself doing nothing
Sitting on nonsense clubby feet
Four inches wider that they ought

Never mind
Sideboard is nobody's ordinary sidekick
That wall space is safely his.

Down the River to the Sea

It's Ruth and the hill
I've found them again
And Ruth is eighty-two now
Bitter Parkinson wants her
But I see her presiding still
Czarina of School Street Hill

Down the hill to the river to the sea

Only one lady-in-waiting
Pictures of her dogs perform the guard
Her court
The bay window of her Victorian mansion
House to hill   the great granite wall holds

Down the hill to the river to the sea

She's the matron
Gave the world four sons of intellect
Two Boston professors
But they left no heir
No one to inherit the hill

And that's the life I see slipping
Down the hill past the State House
To the Merrimack to the sea

Ruth held Valance
They held four sons
Now Val is mindless
Ruth is bodyless

Down the hill to the river to the sea

Nobody's left for the hill
Knows neither comings nor goings
Knows it's time that sits at the top
Knows everything is in waiting
Ruth may be in waiting for what
Is already hers
Eighty-two years
Ruth

Down the hill to the river to the sea.

Justice In the Sky?

A dark form passed over the ground
I had to look up to see what shadow
Hawk wings   wide as two screen doors
Rows of clever underneath feathers
Pale as the sky is gray at dusk

He was weaving   diving   maneuvering
Under attack from the rear
Like a Sopwith Camel trying to escape
The Red Baron in his Messerschmitt

But the enemy wasn't an armed biplane
He was a tiny black barn swallow
And his mate   on the offensive
Little David after a Goliath

The steel blue sky
Is mercilessly neutral.

Being At Bartlett's   Small Point, Maine

More windows than walls
More doors than windows
That's what gets you outside
But outside's already inside

And the ocean's done got you anyway
If it's not whitecaps
It's those little lobster boats
Binoculars show you the lobsterman
Pull traps up   drop them down

Stare at Mt. Washington dawn to dusk
Just naked eyes   gets you eye-drunk
Waves don't mind if you watch
Double back   do it again

Out   the paths say come
To the low tide rocks
Tide pools   pollywogs
Periwinkles mussels snails

Careful   wind will blow you over
Why not
This is just the place to let go
And be blown away.

Rainy Day at Small Point, Maine

Rain I don't mind
You belong
Maybe you came before us anyway

Exciting to watch rain fall
Big drops splat
And that's the end
Of their drama

It'll just get soaked up
By the hungry ground
Puddle in a parking lot

Land in a bog
A maternity ward
For pollywogs tadpoles mosquitos

The desert gets her share seldom
Who decides where to flood
Hold off on rain for Rosemary's wedding

The Queen's garden party
Pour it on in the 7th inning
Red Sox ahead of the Yankees 6 to 5

Put on your Wellies   yellow slicker
That old fisherman's hat
Get out in it
Smell the rain.

Ode To Wool

They've done it to sheep again
Strip that's what
But I'm so glad
I like the standing grace of sheep

They're a picture in my mind
Sheep and wool
I wear it every time

Lory sits beside me
Equal grace in her gray wool dress
Matching wool sweater

The warm room says
Slip it off
Swing it across the chair

Now for the sheep
Wool off in the spring
Cool for the summer heat
New wool for fall

Or nursery rhymes
Little Bo Peep has lost her sheep
They always make everything
Right or everything wrong.

But for the problem
They haven't solved
Polyester the imposter.

Ode to the Trash Can

Mover and remover
I'll woo you a little
Dance around your can can
Precious receptacle of no respect

Alone in the night
Left on the roadside
Garbage overflowing
Flies, gnats, honeybees

No dignity, immobile
Awaiting redemption but
You're not going anywhere
Next week they'll hoist you up

Dump you out
Slam you down

The dance of the can can
A sad one.

Ode to Silence

Out of nothing   God
The glory of the nothing
The noise of nothing
When everything goes silent

A blank sheet of paper
Stuck in a typewriter
What is the book inside of

Winter silence   the industry
Inside a peach tree
A tree making its rings
A chick growing inside an egg

The night that does not say
The energy it takes to raise the sun
When the wind is not blowing

The man in the moon
A newborn   his only
Speak is the eyes of the look

The noise of quiet   when
The electricity goes off
Listen for the sound of the rock
Hear this poem when it ends.

Ode to Dr. Caldwell

I wanted the last good bye
To an old professor
He may be the last great teacher
Enough intensity for the whole department
He had soul to give away.

If ants had a king
Instead of a queen
All the student ants would be
Crawling over his anthill

He would remember them
And bless them one by one
As I have been blessed.

Men's Conference

My lamp has been lit and
I am burning
Die
I think I could
At peace
In the circle of men

I've come to the I am
I have come into the presence of men
And they unto me
I can go now
I may be the oldest man here

I look around
No
I can see a man older than I am
He can lead

I'll wait
Then I will lead the way and
Will the last man to leave
Please blow out the candles.

Castle

If we dedicate mountaintops
To the dance of the gods
Then the hills own themselves
Sacred for the people

Castle is the tall the proud
But didn't take the pinnacle
Is seated with humility
Like where the hare lay

Yields the crown to the primacy
And sanctity of hill
And said much obliged
We'll dignify each other

Men hammers nails saws mud
Hill didn't come down to get it
Castle was pushed up piece by piece
And won't slide down

Because stone footings and bedrock met
That archetypal place where
Where we're all rock
So much minerals

Blessed
Is the castle luxurious
Five or six stories all the way
To the captain's walk
To the sky

But Castle is not a hubris
Is a quiet honor to her contract
With forest's wood she borrowed
Boards sawn and planed

Rings for the passages of time
Like a painted portrait
Where growth traveled
From earth to root
In sacred routes of nourishment

Castles don't bargain   they power themselves
To mountain tops rivers sea sides
With the heaviness of stone

This castle of wood knows
Someday it will return
To the earth   the forest who gave
It on loan to flesh and blood

All will return to the dust
From which it came
Like a precious book borrowed
From the library of time
With a return due date.

Dance of the Silky Sari

It was watermelon country
But the eatery of the Mexicans
Was where they met, the Americans
These men of devoted acquaint
Known for measuring and writing
The accents of their lives in poetry
The six, The last
With white hat came late

I don't know whether God questioned
Before bringing Eve
But the men did
And voted even
To bring the wife of one
Even though her first meeting to eat
Fouled by the rain at the sidewalk café

They moved for her
To sachet into her central place
Under the swirl of the silky sari
Her hand had made

The café she danced her song
And played her hand
That opened and moved the moist and the dry
She teased and they laughed

'Til the swelling bowl overflowed
And the last I saw
Of the circle of men
Of serious acquaint

The bowl of integrity survived
The dance of the silky sari
And they read from the poets.

By the Banks of the River Charles

Late summer and Boston
Such a cool still morn
Not even enough breeze
To stir the water   nor move the
Abandoned sailing skiffs with bare
Masts sticking up like flagless flagpoles
As if all is well and waiting

By the banks of the Charles
We sat to contemplate the flow
To be truthful we couldn't tell
If it was ebb or flow or tide

We were old men contemplating
Old men can do that

The confusion of the tide
Of a young man
Trying to become who he is
When his gravity is adrift
Unable to control his ebb or flow

Is the story of his youth
The memoir
As he read

The onrush of life is impatient   unforgiving
Putting question marks   like
White chalk on the blackboard of his life
Saying do it right now

To get there   over the bridge
Damn signs say jump
Some say don't

Now the bridge is over
He closed that chapter
We were contemplating
Old men can do that

But we never knew if the
Charles was ebb or flow or tide.
It did not matter.

Swing

I love it when 3 guitar players
Fiddle around   tuning up
It's the Spring Gathering
Facing the best of men   us

I love it when my stomach tightens
Up to cry wet in my eyes
I have come unto myself
But don't want to cry now
In front of all these men

Gregory   Simon   Vaughn
On that flat plywood stage
Of unstable pine 2x6's

Life is an unstable one
Like a swing attached
To a high elm limb
By long ropes waiting to be
Swung as high as it will go.

Bud

I know you had a whale of a career
Waterspouts and all   You can measure
Your life in   daughters, college prof
War   hanging Hitler's generals
Walking up the steps of Washington

Who told you not to risk
He was a fool   I think he was
The same one who said you can't
Grow plants like General Electric
IBM Glaxo from seed packets

On abandoned rutted red clay
Piney woods surrounded by
Colleges fertile but fallow
Spliced between
Territory claimed by the KKK
And the Bible Belt on Tobacco Road

Now black birds and Poe birds
Knock your chamber door
The turkey buzzards want to take over

You'll say
    What are you doing here
    I'm busy living the poetry of life
    Go away   Come back some other day.

Perpetuity

The same is always
and the day has been long.
Old men at the seaside.
They come to the boardwalk
and sit on the wooden benches.

They come from far
to spit into the ocean.
No one notices their tiny spit bubbles
nor the men who wear caps with bills
and don't talk.
They are there for days
and no one misses them.

The men who fish
have a purpose.
The men who don't fish
            and don't spit,
            their wives always come to get them.
They will be back next year.
The men who fish never leave.

When Gregory Played His Flute

At the place where men meet
Plastic seated them
When Gregory played his flute
But the serenade of the woodwind
Lulled them to the waters
Where they cannot drink
Without muddy knees.
That's the way men go to pain
Down.

Much has come from simple mud
Jesus in dust spat
And a man could see.
Good dirt and water. Seeds.
Earth is our much-favored planet
There is no end.

Light follows light
Sprouts always go up
When the breath of the flute
Awakens spring on the earth
One more time.

The Handkerchief

I watched Wilson McCreary fold his handkerchief
And place it in his back pocket.
Quietly, it absorbed his tears and
Asked no questions.

Handkerchief.
That's the way they are and
Always have been: soft,
Absorbent,tactile, bending to my will,
Like an extension of me,
From arm to hand to my back pocket
To touch with relief.

Handkerchief.
It was made for tears, blood,
Boogers, snot, dirt, whatever,
Receives my precious body fluids.

We have a sacred contract
That Kleenex can never replace.
If you're not careful
A tissue will rip in your hand
And you're smeared.
Tissue is such a flimsy word.

Handkerchief.
It's cotton, is faithful, and strong,
And after soap and water,
Just comes back for more.
Some of mine are over fifty years old
And have a neat G. B. my mother
Printed in the corner to keep them
Separate in the wash.

Jamaholic

I'm not a chocoholic
I'm a jamaholic
Fig muscadine damson
Sourwood honey on my whole wheat
Biscuits, pancakes, oat bran waffles.
Don't give me bleached flour
Preservatives, dough softeners
Additives, and mono-dote-on-him
Glue to catch a mate.

Give me a 100% stone ground whole grain man
Unadulterated
With wild man seed
Grown in high-potency virgin soil.
Then organic Phoenixes will fly
Out of the violent ash heaps
Of the twentieth century
To make strawberries grow on I-95.

Crook's Corner

If Crook's Corner is a café
Who made her entrance look like a back door
Why all those fake pigs stuck on everything
Like some roadhouse

Proclaiming a big Barbeque hogwash
At Carrboro's front door
You all know Carrboro is Chapel Hill's back door.

Chapel Hill is front door to everywhere
To everything worldly
They all want to go in
Feed at the learning trough
Never come out

'Cept the abandon of 1865
White chalk on the blackboard
Yankees wrote
"This old University's gone to Hell."

Whole Foods Emporium

It's an open-ended open-season
Town gown old young baby-in-
Carriage relaxed busy like a market
Day in a medieval village

Eating drinking hot cold
Hawking wares buying selling
Passing coins gold silver

No need for caveat emptor
Everything's guaranteed
Organic sanforized pre-shrunk
No counterfeit no fooling

Only thing missing minstrels
Fiddlers poets puppets drummers
Dancers buglers clowns
Mimes thieves pick-pockets.

Tattoo Talk

Weaver Street Market
Provident powerhouse café
To the Chapel Hill proletariat
Where wearers of tattoo
Meet at sidewalk tables

To sip strong coffee and herbal teas
Under oversized French market umbrellas
They munch natural goodies
And endow cutting-edge conversation

Say the unmarked
What a distance from here to there
I sit inside
The transparency of the glass
Lets me see what I can't hear
I draw my own pictures

Tattoos
Some say of heaven
And some say of hell
Some say they are openings to the us
That we can't look back at

Saint Paul talks about seeing through glass darkly
And then face to face
We shall behold as we are beheld

Tattoo may be the painted stamp
Of soul on display
Soul seeking light
Perhaps paint sealing soul in
And if the tattoo could talk.

Weaver Street Market II

Prozac for the proletariat,
You'd never think an old cotton mill
Reinvented could stir up so much juice.
I go to her in a lousy mood.
I get the cure.

Salt-of-the-earth people in
Weaver Street, Carrboro's front yard,
Organic overloads looking
For something to create,
Something to abolish.
Rebels in training

All they need is a soap box,
And some proclaimer would be up on it,
Like London's Hyde Park.
Some look like serious students,
Spread out with thick textbooks
And laptop computers.

People eating and chatting
Under two huge wedding tents,
Looking like a nineteenth century
French Impressionist painting.

That's where I want to be
When I get old,
Still in the rush of it,
Dancing organic,
In and out of Weaver Street Market.

Telephone Pole Democracy

Out the cafe window
Leftover pieces of paper
Pinned to a phone pole
Thumb-tacked and stapled
Little pieces of democracy
Written words of free speech
Proclamations of people-power

Vote For Me
Come to Church Supper
Get Your Dog Vaccinated

A creosote-soaked cypress shaft
Sprouts no green leaves
Just dangling black wires
Hang like cheap jewelry

As the world passes by
Cars, trucks, buses
Spew out black fumes
People are going places
Some even returning
Some never got there
Where are you?

American Indians may have camped
Under this tree
They roasted a buffalo
Before the sun went down
Sun's not needed now
Pole holds a street light.

Change slides down the telephone pole.
Through the window
Beware   change will eat you up
You'll just be a streak
Splat
Like a mosquito on a windowpane
You can be wiped away
With Windex and a paper towel.

Durham Farmers Market

It's an edible barn dance
In and out the stable
Where the green grass
Grows all around all around

Where the string Band plays
But nobody calls the squares
    They just roam dance
    In and out the crowds

Bumping into babies
Sweaty armpits between
Cleavage   those low-cut
Bosoms they wear now

Fruits vegetables that's
Where color was invented
Tomatoes red yellow purple
Green ones you take home to
Batter-fry the green way

All the flowers you'll ever need
From christening to wedding to death
Here they are in a bucket of water

Fried apple pies fudge   whole
Wheat home baked basil bread
Goat butter to spread on it
Goat bones for stew

Chops lamb chops pork chop chops
Home baked hamburger buns
Mustard relish pickles

Market Day as ancient
As leaving the Garden
To celebrate provident tenders
Of the soil

Look in their eyes
Touch their hands
Do more than pass dollars
Bless them.

Pickett House

Sitting high on Solterra Hill
Soaking up the sun
At the juncture
Where an old Indian trading route
And Solterra pathways come together.

Just humans seeking to be suns of God
Making sacred their slice of earth
Vowing to share the sun's warmth.

Take a walk to the garden.
Rest a while in the gazebo.
Listen to green bean gossip
And sweet potato poems.

Sample a ripe fig
While the children
Make you a mud pie.

Solterrans want no grass on the pathways.
They're digging for ideals
Where all paths lead
To Pickett Common House.

When I last saw them
Each had found a little piece.
They'll fellowship in Pickett Common House
And put their pieces together.

Vesper Concert at Duke Chapel

Seated on the hard oak pew in Duke Chapel
I heard the chamber orchestra accompany
The Vespers Ensemble sing in Latin verse
Dietrich Buxtehude's 1680
"Membra Jesu Nostri" blessed by the resplendent
Chapel acoustics just on loan from heaven

While sitting five rows ahead of me I had to see a woman's
Head of auburn-dyed hair, and clothed in a paisley blouse
Printed with gray, white, and black figures except for
A small strip of white shoulder skin showing
But a straight shot ahead of her, like looking

Through one of those shotgun houses they have
In New Orleans, you wouldn't believe,
Was a woman wearing an identical blouse,
With a man's blue shirted arm anchoring each to
Each and caressing her biceps in music time,

While the black-suited conductor waved on
With arms like a windmill to start stop shush the choristers'
Breath channeled through their pharynx larynx
Vocal cords passing by teeth over tongues
But not without finally the lips shaping

And exalting the sound that blended on its way upward
Past the oaken carvings to the Gothic arched heights
Penetrating painlessly through the gray limestone
Vaulted ceiling straight into the presence of God.

Black History Poetry Reading

At the Black History Poetry Reading
They bring sweet potatoes
In Styrofoam covered plates

She pushes the plastic fork
To divide the butterbeans
From the green peas

The tongue pushes the yams
But they stop
To stand
Long enough to read their poems

My color is uneasy

Two scoops of ice cream
    vanilla and chocolate
    left on her plate
    melt and run together

Reminds me of ice cream parlors
They have soda jerks
    thick milk shakes
    dark brown chocolate syrup
    milk
    vanilla ice cream

It makes a whir-r-r
    buzz-z-z
    clank-clank
    metal-against-metal
    that stainless steel cup

Finished at last
He pours it
    a big Dixie cup
    the last stroke
    sticks a straw

The rest
Slurp
I don't even have to tell you

Ice cream
    the world's favorite food
    eat it
    drink it
All at the same time.

Head Nurse

She's the Baccalaureate of the University
The head of her class
As serious as the creased brow
Of the Sphinx

In Egypt's fabled land
Presiding over the mysteries
Of year-swept sands

I'm waiting
For the Sphinx to rise
Lift her skirts
Not to scurry away downtown

But to say
Let's dance
As brown people do
In desert heat.

After

It must be like this
The people have   come and gone
As it should be

Like snow comes in winter
Then it melts and is gone
As it should be

It was so pretty
Covered all
In winter the wonder is
Will spring ever come

Now is both cover and uncover.

Taken

When you take me
Let it be
Down the road

Through the woods
Where it winds
Turn to the left

Woods in winter
Lets you see forever
A forever right for the day

Lanes lead off
Don't tell you where
Not even who

They wind like the curve
Of the earth   in silence
Some gates will be closed.

Pass

Will I pass
I'm going to die
English gives us that good word dead
No euphemism ism

Let the medical students
Peel and scrape for reusable scraps
Then with or without ceremony
Burn me on the blackbird pyre

The buzzards will kettle
The downdrafts and updrafts

I want a funeral
Not a sanitized Celebration of Life
Funeral is final

For weeping and wailing
Import professional mourners
From Bangladesh Pakistan Viet Nam

Let the drummers rattle tight skins
Noise up to the rafters
Sing the great hymns

Read poems
That stroke the heart
Some words will be mine

Then someone will stand up and say
This is enough.

Last Will And Testament

Cremate me
But I want a funeral
Memorial service doesn't
Sound like forever
Funeral is final

And I want to be there
To listen to what they say about me
Let there be much good music
One vase of flowers

How many will weep and wail
The way I cried my life and my poems
Surely my ashes will weep
At my funeral

No fancy brass urn nor Tupperware
The undertaker my ancestor
John Edward Bell Shutt made coffins
I won't need one
Just a little wooden box

Give the ashes to the
Wind in Solterra's garden
This feels so painfully final
Like a wound in my chest

These things always end with
Cookies baked at home
Triangular chicken salad sandwiches
Made with whole grain bread
They cut the crust off

Stalks of celery stuffed
With pimento cheese
Don't make watery punch
With ginger ale and a blob
Of green sherbet floating

Give them a good coffee
Like I'd want to drink

You can buy some wine
My children are like that
Loving them came easy
There are no doubts

I always wanted Betty Bell
To paint a portrait of Alice
She deserved that and more
Than she got from me

Her teachers said
She could be famous
If we spent enough $

My portrait hangs
Over the mantel
Her best student painted it
Look at me.

Grady Bennett Myers, Jr., Tar Heel born, English major at UNC, but did not begin writing until the nineties prompted by Coleman Barks and the Men's Movement. He lived years in New Hampshire and writes about granite and the rocky coast of Maine, nature, and his Southern heritage and Grandpa poems. Look for passion, connection to people, and subtle wit in drawing out the richness of the past and present.